M000015079

LEARNING TO BE HUMAN

OTHER BOOKS BY LESTON HAVENS

Approaches to the Mind
Participant Observation
Making Contact
A Safe Place
Coming to Life

LEARNING TO BE HUMAN

LESTON HAVENS, M.D.

A William Patrick Book

Addison-Wesley Publishing Company
Reading, Massachusetts   Menlo Park, California   New York
Don Mills, Ontario   Wokingham, England   Amsterdam   Bonn
Sydney   Singapore   Tokyo   Madrid   San Juan
Paris   Seoul   Milan   Mexico City   Taipei

Library of Congress Cataloging-in-Publication Data

Havens, Leston L.
    Learning to be human / Leston Havens.
       p.   cm.
    "A William Patrick book."
    ISBN 0-201-62474-5
    1. Conduct of life   2. Autonomy (Psychology)
   3. Compliance I. Title
    BF637.C5H35 1994
    158' .1 — dc20   93-43261
                                           CIP

Jacket design by Suzanne Heiser
Text design by Karen Battles
Set in 13.5 - point Centaur by Battles Design

1 2 3 4 5 6 7 8 9-ARM-97969594
First printing, February 1994

To Gregg, Peter, Grace:
For Having Enlarged Our Human Ground

My thanks for Marguerite Yourcenar's *Memoirs of Hadrian*, Joseph Conrad's first great *Preface*, Joseph Solman's *Mozartiana*, Edward Hundert's gift for structure, and Myron Sharaf's genius for quotation, which gives him access to the spirit of the age.

...woe to the man whose heart has not learned while young to hope, to love —and to put its trust in life.

—Joseph Conrad

CONTENTS

Introduction...I

Trespass...7

A Giant in the Belly of the Whale..............12

Giving and Taking in the Day-to-Day.......20

Friendship...31

Lived Time and Space...................................45

Sexuality..58

Securing Time and Space..............................72

Marriage...88

Divorce...110

Children..118

The Search for the Real..............................127

Naming...129

The Real..137

Death and Dying.......................................144

INTRODUCTION

Today we watch the dawn of the psychological age: for many, physical subsistence has lost its ancient primacy to the goals of personal perspective and self-possession. Demands for individuality and self-expression spring up all around us. People shop at supermarkets of values and ideals that invite deciding "for themselves." Extraordinary new sciences hold the hope of gauging and recording our states of mind. For the first time many feel free to ask: What do I feel? What is for me?

How do I build a life I love with those I love? What makes relationships so difficult and institutions so dangerous? What happens when people fall in love? Can we understand the psychological problems of sex? Or the basis of friendship? What do I possess when I possess myself?

Some problems seem trivial: Can I hang up the phone? Others momentous: Why do people disdain me? Conventions of thought impose feelings of clarity. Then other feelings erupt: anxiety, rage, sadness, as the gap opens between what we thought and the actual. These feelings are diagnosed as sickness or even diseases. But they may only be the body's signals of what we are missing — a viable existence. Is there a map of that human ground?

The central theme of this book is a paradox: *We must be both as free and as compliant as we dare.* Without freedom, compliance is tyranny; without compliance there is only revolt and no freedom. Revolution has not proved useful in this century because it brings the same fury to the solution as produced the problem. This is apparent too on the individual level when dominating persons and creeds, even while they speak of liberation, impose new straitjackets. Most of all, liberty asks of its practitioners respect, even when it is spit upon. Such were the teachings of

Gandhi and King. But how to achieve it in personal relations, in the family, in the state?

To be human precludes perfection or a single chain of being. There are very different races to run: One family gives closeness and harmony within convention, only to produce children who need to learn the lessons of the individual, even the alienated. Another is rich in rebellion, producing children who must find value in convention. No line points to a single future. We have to be ready to tell lies out of self-protection or loyalty, as Orwell wrote, and to be broken by love because we have committed ourselves to others and to ideals.

Every institution is the belly of a whale. How do we survive there? We give and take in the day-to-day. Can we contact one another without distortion and be alone in each other's company when we need to? Friendship is being both close and open. How is this precious opportunity at once fostered and protected in a predatory world? Sexuality exposes humans to their greatest joys and fears: moments of transcendence and ample opportunities for humiliation and loss — nothing so tests the human capacities for both giving and possessing ourselves. Marriage is a statement of the bravest bet humans place on one another—to live and build together through an unbounded future. How can that dedication be protected throughout its life? Above all, when we give and possess ourselves, what is it we give and possess?

※

The paragraphs that follow are separated so the reader will not be hurried nor a strong continuity expected or imposed. I want reading this book to illustrate its message—to be treated humanly is to find a time and a space of one's own.

Conrad, Nietzsche, Cézanne, Aristotle, some others, are quoted because their understanding of the human makes them like the

most original of mathematicians, able to provide intuitive results that need lifetimes to
grasp and test. In this guide to the human
ground, inspired by their example, I mean
to shape a vision for these new, psychological
times.

TRESPASS

1

■

I can walk on your land if I secure your permission and practice respect of its contents. These simple rules do not now obtain between minds.

■

The result is: Human beings are trespassed on, their spirits hurt or crushed, many oblivious. And the intruders go their way unchecked.

■

A physical analogue for psychological trespass is the drunk driver: someone of clouded perspective propelling a dangerous instrument. The most common psychological instances are convictions of rightness driving powerful opinions. Convictions of rightness denote a clouded perspective whenever those convictions address areas for which only opinion and uncertainty are appropriate. Such areas include almost all of what people say about each other. Powerful opinions are essentially conventional opinions—that is, views backed by strong traditions with large bodies of often frantic adherents.

The concept of trespass in our culture is not now extended to these psychological acts of driving to endanger or assault with a deadly weapon because our ideas of "mine" and "yours" are largely restricted to physical property and do not include subjective spaces and times that should be equally respected. I refer to acts of aggression which are personally directed, as when *I* tell *you*. The reader can throw this book aside, with indifference or joy. Try that on your boss, or on your parents.

Psychological trespass is easiest to see with young people whose space is treated as a common ground into which I can push my ideas of what a person must be, thin, quiet, married, above all "nice".

Or I can sense your individuality and your promise, hold it for a moment in my contact with you, treasure it.

Because there are no public trials for psychological trespass, we can only describe suspects, and that chiefly by their effects on us. Students of the jurisprudence of the future, finding the present efforts rudimentary, may turn the variety of human collisions into a new forest of torts. But the many victims of the legal system itself can hope instead for habits of civility, which is the dream of these paragraphs.

The sad fact is, objects of psychological assault are far better described than their assailants. This is not surprising since the victims are the ones brought for examination and help. Worse yet, many are assaulted afresh by the descriptions. Victims are told they selected or designed the collisions, perhaps out of masochistic impulses. I suspect the assailants are once again in charge, this time of defining the terms.

Can we accept that everyone carries a solitary viewpoint, staring forth from our individually shaped and genetically different nervous systems onto a world glimpsed from this spot by no one else? Behind that pinprick, like a flashlight putting forth its tiny trail of light, how we need each other's vision!

As we learn to understand our human nature, as we see we need our own space and each other, the conditions of a viable existence become as compelling as the physical and financial threats that now preoccupy us. Aware of psychological destructiveness, we are already a little armed against it, and can find the comfort and the place to hope, to love, and to put our trust in life.

A GIANT IN THE BELLY
OF THE WHALE

Many feel as giants to themselves, the way objects that are closest seem largest. They may not know they are confined and being psychologically digested.

Entering institutions, young people are like those giants in the whale. The first contact can be friendly; the greeter is leaving and therefore at the door, or an outcast in need of friends. Anthropologists, too, will be welcomed by these pariahs of the tribe.

Insiders know. Watching from a balcony or an office at the center of empire, insiders know. They are often the same insiders who were deposed two months before. You can see them on playgrounds, standing tall, the objects of glances.

What do insiders know? They know who the insiders are. Consider the system of money. Money is the supreme tool for conventionalizing value; by money we are immediately told "what something is worth." Money therefore permits entry to the system. Spending a great deal means conversing with insiders: you can talk on their terms. The real cost is, as Wilde said, we end knowing only the price and never the value.

Insiders grasp the structure of conventions not yet reduced to money terms and therefore still outside common perception. People know when they are poor. But the unperceived structure of conventions allows people to be ruled even while they feel free.

Power rests on the perception of having power. Few are willing to test it, either by free thought or free action. They soon discover that the public mind is owned just as the land is owned, but by conventional opinions. Insiders embody or manage these opinions and are prepared to pay for them with their life—but more often with the lives of those who obey them.

Young people stepping cheerfully into human institutions must work hard at what the bosses value, to the point of becoming indispensable. *Indispensable* means that the institution needs them more than they need it.

Still, watch the bosses. Every institution is the belly of a whale. The very boss that hired you is also inside the whale. Isn't he being digested? Is there an independent spirit anywhere?

Outsiders learn they are outsiders by observing insiders. Many insiders will not tell you what they think. Watch their eyes. Approaching outsiders, they turn aside. Friendship, too, avoids the sensitive, but that is out of love. Insiders are thinking: you are impossible. Then they look aside.

Digestion means the slow breakdown of personal unity into common human elements that can circulate safely throughout the whale. Love and loyalty work best, but even hatred and envy circulate safely because they will be neutralized by threats or bribes. What insiders fear is self-possession, since those who possess themselves can defend themselves and possess others, including the insiders.

Survival without slavery depends upon the courage to be both free and compliant. If you are not free, others will digest you. If you are not compliant, there is only revolt and no time for freedom: you are too busy storming barricades, seeking shelter, binding your wounds. Psychological health rests on the balance point between freedom and compliance.

Tip in either direction and anger or depression appears. A life of revolt surrenders freedom to fury because few natures have the harmony to be alone and in opposition without copying their enemies. This is the fate of revolutionary movements everywhere: opposites come to resemble one another in their single-mindedness, complementary tyrannies of "right" answers. On the other hand, compliance suffers depression. Instead of organizing around opposition, the compliant embrace and absorb what they come to hate, then end by hating themselves.

Many exist on a small diet of freedom and compliance. They don't feel safe to be their own or another's. The result is ennui. They are going through the motions.

I must be both as free and as compliant as I dare. I must explore the outer reaches of both independence and loyalty. My model will be Lincoln, who seemed as hard as granite and as soft as a cloud. I will learn to be as strong and as weak as I need to be.

Each feeds the other. I cannot comply whole-heartedly until I am my own person. I cannot be free without the strength of others.

The wise one knows that he or she cannot fight every battle. The amiable one does not want to. Both freedom and compliance are therefore double-games in which I need you for the next battle and you need me for yours. The balance point is found only over time. One's personal history, perhaps history in general, like a ship at sea, moves across the point of equilibrium as it comes about.

When is the trimmer of sails merely a trimmer? I too suffer thoughts of the countless poor for whom I do nothing. Meantime I am short-tempered even toward those close to me, for whom I feel love. Here too we need a balance point, between the distant and the near.

We want to be at home and not be owned, to belong without being belongings. Therefore we need something of our own and something others can make their own. I want to be with you and to help you find what is yours alone. Society and solitude.

All that follows speaks at once to the demands and to the concessions we must make, in this learning to be human.

Conrad wrote, "Few men realize that their life, the very essence of their character, their capabilities and audacities, are only the expression of their belief in the safety of their surroundings." So we take up the study of those surroundings.

GIVING AND TAKING
IN THE DAY-TO-DAY

Your telephone call rings in my space and then takes my time. Do you ask if I am "free"? If not, there is an assumption of my being available, waiting on the call, like a waiter. And am I free to hang up?

Time and space may be mine to give, and become yours to take. The very poor, who have little space and often much time, can show their temporal riches in the form of a waiting courtesy to the often impatient rich. This is an aspect of lived time and space: to exist in relationship to another's time and space, pushed aside by it, invaded, or the two met and enriched.

Many hurry to reach the next red light. Watch them give you time as they take your space.

Perhaps I cannot be alone with you. I feel your silence as a reprimand: my time and space are invaded by this fancied slight. Or in fact, you will not let me be alone. Anxious, you ask, "Am I displeasing you?" Some are not even free to think their own thoughts, lest they leave the other unattended. This is part of what people call being "pulled out of shape."

Or: I am alone in my airplane seat until a vibrant, colorful person sits next to me. My space is unsettled, my time suddenly pressed (although nothing has been said). The bright colors of the other's space fall on me like nothing else; I want so quickly to look and please. I am giving myself away, which goes all the way from revealing my motives to being possessed.

A surprising number are unable to keep anything for themselves; such is experienced as selfish or inconsiderate. They signal unmistakably the expectation of attack and surrender. Others take and keep everything for themselves. The two types coexist efficiently until one is crushed out of existence altogether or the other becomes bored with these easy conquests. Even slight imbalances set in motion remarkable changes.

Some have little time and space themselves which they value enough to remain within; they move in with others. This can be done so subtly that the invaded is unaware: the invader becomes a creature of the other's imagination. A photographer of Marilyn Monroe remarked that it was unnecessary to tell her how to pose or where to stand; she appeared wired in to the other's intentions.

(Monroe remarked that she was a different person with everyone she met.) The ability to take up an imaginative existence in another person's mind, while appearing to be in one's own body, can be immensely attractive: the other's hoped-for future (what are called wishes) is embodied. There is a great empowering of the wishers—natures otherwise docile and hesitant become strong and confident. But the Monroes of this world! Adored, sought after, yet prisoners. Suicide follows naturally on this impoverishment of the human.

Some patients move into therapists' minds. I knew one young person who made her most hesitant helpers certain of every diagnosis and interpretation. She, too, wanted to die.

The same process in marriage makes decisions easy: one may want to please the other, and therefore empowers him or her. People go for years doing things neither wants but each has imagined.

The capacity to live inside what is not one's own is called impostorship and associated with antisocial behavior. But the great bulk of impostors are actually compliant, living within conventions they have never made their own. They are possessed by rather than possess roles sometimes deeply alien. This is not to deny that a certain false affability and politeness is a necessary social lubricant, but such white lies stand far apart from an automaton-like going-through-the-motions by people who have never taken possession of themselves.

Others are captives to attention: they cannot send their mind anywhere. Some have told me that they were early trained to attend, by threats of parental madness or attack. I suspect the mind can be lost when it ultimately flees this constant watch.

A century ago extreme compliance was tested in the clinics by saying "put out your tongue" and then striking the tongue with a pin. A few patients went on obeying while their tongue was a bloody pulp. It is a nice medical test: you can count the strikes.

Respectful meeting therefore confronts possibilities of obedience, fearfulness, being overpowered, or the other setting up shop in one's mind. And your respecting my freedom does not mean I respect yours.

I give you time, as I wait. At least momentarily you become my future. I give you space, perhaps literally standing back. In friendship we mingle our times and spaces. In sexuality we sometimes fuse them. Marriage is the proposal of a joint construction. In all our comings-together perhaps the best test of success is this: Can we be alone together—enjoy one another and leave one another alone?

Sharing time is to share a mood because feelings cross even the most closely guarded frontiers. I can stop myself from talking or listening, but feelings express themselves through countless signals with the contagiousness of chicken pox. This makes the determination of moods both easy and difficult: easy because we catch them readily from others but difficult because which is mine and which is yours? Then meeting resembles a busy international airport or the watery boundary between one fisherman and the next.

The experience of receiving another person's feelings without distortion requires a state of lived time and space in which the receiver's mood is put aside and one's space unoccupied; the receiver is briefly nowhere and nowhen. This freeing-up is done imaginatively (by an act of sympathy) and at best partially: one ignores for a period one's own experience and allows entrance to the experience of something alien but acceptable. The inner movement is distinct, as opposed to the automatic and dangerously unthinking acceptance of the vulnerable: I accept what is another's.

Once within my experience, your lived time and space awaits its fate. Will I think it crazy, or touch it gently, reassuringly, or leave it there to continue imagining its own future? Freud stumbled on an invention in this regard as precise as penicillin. His recommendation that analysts disappear, be silent, neutral, anonymous, indeed not attend to any particular part of the patients' associations at all, meant that the patient readily projected on this receptive space the earliest hopes. Moreover, this same silent and unjudging stance meant that all these efforts at restoring the past were frustrated, so that people hesitant but ready to abandon their family expectations had met the exact cure. Penicillin kills bacteria by taking up a position in their cell walls, blocking nutrition. Analysts gain the same position by silence and anonymity; they destroy the infantile expectations by not nourishing them through action. Note the beauty of not attending to anything in particular: the analysts were warned from even the smallest explanation or advice. If the patient actually doesn't need reparenting, here is the essence of respectful meeting.

The bulk of us probably do need reparenting, with the result that respectful meeting had best acknowledge what will otherwise lie in wait. This means encouraging or speaking for what the other cannot say and, oppositely, ignoring or cuffing back what should not be reinforced. Some have a genius for keeping their relationships realistic. Being with them is to feel a straight, steady course, the opposite of "pulled out of shape"—we like the person we are. All of us can draw closer to this ideal by simply attending to how we feel, pulled or pulling, resisting the impulse to collude or control.

Today's technology makes freedom and privacy even harder to find. The telephone has been succeeded by the beeper and the "digital assistant," portable noisy consciences often accessible to anyone in a hurry. Everyday experience then approximates the hallucinated world of independent voices able to harry and surround. We are invaded, even possessed.

Fortunately, few contacts are all-consuming events: most of us can send our mind away. This makes education tolerable. One does not have to listen to everything said but can check in periodically and find little added. (Meantime those attentive, even enthusiastic faces are kept on.) The same saving process protects readers. Ideally, the present author does not hurry after idly musing readers, invading their times and spaces.

I want the reader to feel both attended to and left alone. Once experienced this can be the model for what one seeks in the day-to-day.

FRIENDSHIP

Friendship, in a sense other than acquaintanceship, unites two qualities dangerous
when found together—closeness and openness. I want my friend to be near. I also open
my time and space to his or her scrutiny
and comment. Friendship can therefore be a
hunting license for the predatory.

True friendship, in the sense of a relationship protective of both parties, must as a
result be rare. True friends need that unusu-
al combination of both parties wanting to
be close and at the same time tactful of their
exposure.

The person to whom I give access to my experience must be sensitive to its sensitivities. He or she is in a confined space the tissues of which have in many and surprising places been worn raw. Thus friendship is as remarkable for what is not said as it is for any exchange of confidences. My friend's noticing what I am not ready to share must be concealed behind a graceful not noticing. Otherwise I will feel him watching me from behind his warmth.

In the novel *Shibumi*, Trevanian has the protagonist receive as a gift an important secret from a dying man, who gives it because the protagonist never once mentioned that the man was a midget, even so much as to comment that it didn't matter.

My impression is that men's friendships tend to err on the side of too much silence and protection and women's in the opposite way. I have known women whose "friends" feed off them like barracuda, and men with no friends, or "friends" so little known their suicide was a surprise.

If a particular time was painful, it must be approached gingerly, if at all. That time or place or presence still aches. Only in the springtime of friendship, in what is called chumship, are the two young parties likely to be so virgin of defeat as to move easily in each other's experience. At that time, characters, as well, may be little formed and open to imitation and identification. Both can feel like twins.

So, when people are young, as in school or college, friendships are made the way almost nothing else between humans is made, friendships with a strength that endures growing incompatibilities of temperament and situation. Both friends may even come to feel, how could we ever have been friends? The answer is, because the two can return to the time and space they were in together. Such is the joyful side of reunions, when worlds long gone are for a while reexperienced.

Just as friendship can be based on the past, it can be based on the future: we share a common cause. Then differences are forgotten in the intense, shared futuring. These friendships are more fragile than those based on the past because the future may not be realized together or never come into a settled existence.

For the most part, the chance of such easy friendship fades. Then friends know sensitivities that can only be put aside or approached cautiously. This is the reason "your best friend won't tell you," often something you need to know. The good friend values the friendship more than the state of your dentures or the fate of your marriage, if commenting on either would threaten the friendship.

At this point friendship enters the narrower space of walking together or meeting over lunch. It needs this limitation to prevent what a broader exposure of time and space must thrust into view, an exposure that even the most seasoned tact cannot master.

It needs this limitation to preserve its emotional base in mutual admiration. It is mutual admiration that fuels the closeness and animates the tact: I wish to keep this person the person I love. Amidst all its talk, friendship is a conspiracy of silence.

For this and other reasons friendship between couples is rarer still. As we all talk, what I hear you say to someone else shakes our relationship; it is like listening in on someone's phone. And the statistical likelihood that all four in their various combinations should wish closeness and protect openness approaches the astronomical.

Friendship is seen as a model: for psychotherapy, for relationships with oneself or others (for example, the so-called I–thou), and in sexuality, society, and marriage.

Psychotherapy has been called paid friendship; the reasons for calling it that are instructive, as well as corrective of the snide implication. Psychotherapy, like friendship, embraces both closeness and at least a one-sided openness. Because psychotherapy, unlike friendship, is not equal time, the payment compensates the psychotherapist in part for not being listened to and understood. Further, because friendship is rare and highly valued, people are happy to pay for it. More pointedly still, because many friendships are paid for in ways much more costly than psychotherapy — such as when openness is abused — the cost of psychotherapy comes into a new light. Sadly, though, openness in psychotherapy, too, often stands abused, so some of the differences vanish.

People speak of being their own best friend. Meanwhile we all talk to ourselves. This last fact illustrates why friendship is not easy or even wise in relation to oneself. Certainly people berate themselves, inspire and give advice to themselves. The difficulty of being a friend to oneself (except in the sense of soothing or encouraging oneself) is that one knows too much and in remembering and thinking treats oneself tactlessly; in fact, one needs to treat oneself thus, to dispel sentimental illusions. The closest people get to inner friendship is in neurosis, when a selective amnesia or denial maintains a friendly interior. The price for this is heavy, and often entails being unready and off guard. A certain level of anxiety and regret, as inner ingredients, both maintains realistic attitudes and, as a dividend, gives friendship with others its special joy.

St. Teresa found "a serene dissatisfaction" with herself. I wish my dissatisfaction were serene.

Here is a saving observation: Pompous people often talk to themselves as pompously as they do to others, so that any suffering we experience is shared with them.

Many attempt to make friendship a general model for relationships with others: "I never met a man I didn't like." As a political posture, this sentiment is useful, but if taken with full seriousness, it either degrades friendship to a vigilant acquaintanceship or exposes its defenders to abuse. It is possible for friendship to serve as a model for ideal relationships, as in the concept of I–thou.

This goal of treating others as subjects and not objects is identical with what I have described as true friendship: the other's lived time and space is allowed access to one's experience on its own terms. However, the elevation of ideal relationships to a general social formula tempts people to treat the invasive with excessive respect. One should keep the ideal for the ideal.

Romance combines elements of sexuality and friendship; at its most intense this is called being in love. Psychological closeness and openness then merge with physical attraction and responsiveness to a sometimes explosive result. Only in religious awe and political mass movements is this level of excitement approached. These are all examples of human fusion.

The transient quality of romance is related not only to this intensity but to the perils of closeness and openness, especially when experienced bodily. The difficulties of maintaining oneself under conditions of merger are multiplied by the temptations to bodily conquest and surrender. What is a physiologically determined transient experience of sexuality has attached to it the psychologically shaped hopes of continuance, even permanence. This hope may be still more ambitiously pursued into marriage. While friendships can call on silence, tact, and their spatial equivalents of separation and absence, romance attempts to maintain itself in the incandescence of mental and bodily fusion. This is usually done by the surrender of one party to the other: the assumption of a slave role or a virtual going-out-of-one's-own-existence.

Friendship may heighten sexuality in romance; it still more often diminishes it by familiarity and embarrassment. Much of the appeal of prostitutes is their anonymity: This one hardly has a name, at least not a last name; few are known the way friends are known; the whole transaction is enacted by that largely uniform space we inhabit, the body. It may be for this reason that prostitutes, it is said, seldom kiss, in contrast to courtesans: kissing is the smallest bodily remove from conversation. Wilde remarked that nothing so destroys romance as a sense of humor in the partner. The point is that friendship invites a tactful, sometimes humorous, exposure; this is not easily made part of a passionate bodyhood.

Friendship, as an ideal, is not only carried into sexuality and marriage but into ideals of society as a whole. In the movement from solitude to society the step beyond friendship is the club. This is a union of the like-minded, whether the point of similarity is as small as the desire to eat or play golf together or as large as shared values and political ideals. These last become little societies or tribes, and may even grow into nations. The idea of communism—that is, the elimination of barriers of class and property—is the concept of friendship carried to its logical extreme: we are to be close to one another in these respects and not greater or smaller. It is not surprising that the imposition of such ideals on a diverse human nature requires authoritarian power and force. It is an enforced friendship, like the pattern of domination and submission by which closeness is often continued in romance and marriage.

Friendship cannot be the ideal form of marriage either. Marriage is a dangerous sea-crossing, often with many passengers aboard and a sometimes divided crew: tact is important but not always desirable. If your best friend won't tell you, your spouse must be able to. In this respect marriage is more like one's relationship with oneself than like friendship. Tact must sometimes give way to a saving ruthlessness.

LIVED TIME AND SPACE

A person's present is the occasion when the future both comes into and goes out of existence: what might be appears or disappears. It functions like a moving and working centrifuge, selecting from the possibilities of human existence the lived present. The movement of this selecting process, in turn, leaves a trail called the past.

The present is the occasion of building past into future. It is also the occasion of future becoming past. (Old people speak of their futures being behind them.) This capacity of the past to move into future and the future into past distinguishes lived time from clock time. The future movement of time through present is exemplified by my taking what I now have and making something different.

But what is newly built is now part of the past. Or nothing may happen, so that while clock time passes, lived time stands still. Because the future keeps entering the present, we have a relationship with it like that with an "intimate stranger."

A big day or great time is a special concentration of possibilities here now, which bequeaths a memorable place.

As one moves into the future by anticipation, one moves into the past by memory. Then the moodedness of time is evident; as one goes back, a mood takes hold. Try changing your mood in the presence of the past. The difficulty is most evident when the past is entered not only by memory but through those aspects of spatial experience that have been past-ed. In different words, the past emerges most vividly in the encounter between mind and world, as when an object reminds us of an event that has happened or itself embodies that event.

The different mooding of one time from another may be so great that the happiness we have at one moment is unimaginable in another. Then we may not even be able to imagine the return of the first. Fortunately this is also true of pain, less often of unhappiness.

As time comes mooded, space comes colored and scented and sounded. Cézanne is rumored to have said, "Color is the point at which brain meets world," but he was not a cook, who smells and tastes the world, or a musician. Space exposes the sensational, whether a mountain or some sexual or gastronomic delight. One's mood may be changed forever in hope or despair of such a return.

Thus the mooding of time and the coloring of space express what is central to human life. Every effort to escape mood and sensation, whether in abstractions or by scientific or political controls, ends where it began, with someone confronting the idea or the experiment in a certain mood with a certain sensation.

Even art, which makes the supreme effort to fix mood and sensation in a timeless form of its created space, still confronts a timebound audience in its own space. Yet the power of great art is such as to transform the very perspectives brought to bear on it, as the new art becomes accommodated into the conventional viewpoints of its audience.

What did Mendelssohn mean, that music is the language of the emotions? It is the subtlety of those reverberations, so much more various than any written account of emotions. Once my wife heard Leontyne Price, in a store, suddenly begin to sing. It was as if the great voice had begun to cry, with an almost infinitely greater depth and subtlety of feelings than weeping. These feelings had been represented, the way color can be represented in a painting, inescapably to an audience caught unaware.

Her music was unexpected, with the effect of coming suddenly on an overpowering picture. Such is the nature of the unexpected future, which can empower even trivial events through surprise. In contrast, an anticipated catastrophe is discounted. A great part of psychological stability is freedom from the unexpected. For this reason most try to live closely ordered lives.

Because the movement both into the future and into the past can occur only through the changing present, both anticipation and memory are subject to revision. Put differently, because the future is feeding and changing the present, the perspective from which the past is seen changes. Therefore each generation rewrites history and biography.

"That seems ages ago." "But it was only yesterday." "I can remember it as if it were yesterday." The past of lived time extends beyond clock time, or is shortened, on the model of spatial perspective. If I look behind me from a hilltop, I can see back until a higher hill intrudes. An event seems ages ago when much of greater magnitude has occurred since; being out of sight it is almost out of time. On the other hand, the last great event looms just behind, if nothing so large has come between. For this reason, people's experiencing can end with their last great event, so that old people often live on the mountaintops of long ago. In the same way, waiting stretches time, until something happens: the present is extended, as a distant horizon is farther off than one made by the house next door. The "cure" of painful events is therefore most decisively other events, and people to whom little happens are subject to destructive arrests.

Presence is the spatial interface of body and the world. As past and future move into each other, so body can move into the world through presence and the world into body, as when we eat. We can also experience spatial stillness (meantime, lived time may be racing, as in anticipation of a movement).

Just as the present is the occasion of building past into future, so presence occasions building in the world or building the world of the body. This is illustrated by another sport, golf, which, like bodybuilding itself or baseball, is an untimed sport (but what they surrender in temporal structure, they take back by counting). Watch a great golfer like Jack Nicklaus control his body's impact: a rapidly moving presence manages exquisitely controlled effects on a tiny ball now sailing into the world. Earlier that world itself had been elaborately built to site this contest between body and world. One plays in space, as the sculptor plays with space.

The spatial experience of future entering present is often a throwing. The sperm is thrown into the womb, the child into the family, the young person into the world. By this is meant not always a literal throwing, but in the sense of throwing dice, of a gamble or unpredictable combination, like an accident. The appearance of a new thing in the present is not simply the addition of one thing to another but is experienced as a collision or a disappearance, or sometimes, and perhaps most remarkably, as nothing at all.

The past expresses itself spatially as ground-edness and rootedness. Just as the ground is geologically the accretion of the past, so what the individual has built is the foundation of further movement. In school years the term *graded* is used, to express the measured ascent. Insofar as the ascent is more than a matter of piling one level on top of another, there are living connections among the steps and one speaks of rootedness. The living connections nourish present action: one has not simply graduated but carried vital elements forward. Human roots do more than nourish; they are like plant roots capable of themselves deepening. This is experienced humanly in the discovery that what one has learned in the past deepens its meaning, for example that what once seemed superficial or useless has profound implications. Here, again, the past is reexperienced.

One wants to give oneself and those with whom one dwells a past that will nourish them. Thus a dwelling implies marks of accretion, like the earth. A stranger knows you dwell here because in pictures, mementos, and, above all, what are called keepsakes, the accreting past is memorialized. Of course the past can become so heavy it prevents movement: each generation of famous families must tear itself free so as not to be cemented in the past.

Watch free children shape their own space. This one's room is covered in drawings or pictures. That one's all in black. When do we let the child with the wildly disordered room find his or her own order, and when do we impose ours?

The past-ing of time and space is experienced as the feeling of familiarity. Even happenings that seem at first unbearable are borne into the past toward a tolerable familiarity. Some who have lost children express surprise that they themselves have survived. They may even talk of what was once unspeakable.

The ground and the past gain their apparent steadiness from being what has settled, in the case of the earth, and in the case of past from being what has reached the present out of all the future possibilities. But in both cases the future may materialize possibilities that destroy the stability of either, as those who live in earthquake country know. I remember a friend of my father's having to relearn his profession because sulfa drugs and penicillin had eliminated any need for the surgery he practiced.

The categories past, present, and future are replaced by beginning, middle, and end when lived time is ordered into a novel or play. Human life itself can be seen in this way if one arranges it like a plot. Then one looks forward to the future, even worships the future in youth, as at the start of a play, and in the end looks back, perhaps worships the past if the life or the play has been good. There is often a crisis in the middle, as one wavers between looking forward or back. Has the past been built well enough so that one can afford to look back when the future shrinks? Or is one caught between an empty past and a closing future? At that point many leave life or walk out of the play.

The same process can be expressed spatially. As soon as humans can stand, they begin to leap, and love to be thrown upward. In midlife they stand on their own. (If not well rooted they can be blown over.) Late in life they lean on others or, as Oedipus knew, on a stick; otherwise they go to ground. One can measure satisfaction in life by the extent to which childhood is safely thrown, middle age has built itself well enough to stand, and the aged have cultivated deeply those they must lean upon. But none of these happy possibilities dictates that we must consistently look forward and move onward, as commencement addresses suggest. A static inwardness is sometimes the occasion for extraordinary building, and many situations, when looking out will only terrify, dictate imitating the ostrich.

As a rule, life is more clock-timed and calendared early than late. There are the school years and one deadline after another. Birthdays gradually lose their specialness until decade marks replace them. Retirement means, in part, unmeasured time. Soon there is only one deadline left, which one awaits. But toward the end one begins to count again, first the years, then the days, finally each breath.

SEXUALITY

Life begins in sexuality, and for many it resumes there too, even the very old. This is because sexuality is the body as both subject and object of desire, feeling and felt. Sensation is fully mobilized by this concentration: seeing, hearing, smelling, tasting, touching, even the sensations of balance and movement are both here and there.

The mobilization is effected by putting all space and time in the service of the body. Presence is transformed seductively: For example, clothing becomes a code of disclosures and concealments of the sexual body that lies beneath. The world itself is centered on giving resonance to the experience anticipated. Bodyhood is doubled. Heterosexuality and homosexuality lose their distinctiveness and both can be played out where man and woman are present: the man is mirrored back to the man in the eyes of the woman, and the woman to the woman.

Temporally, sexuality mobilizes expectation in foreplay, discovers in climax what may have been the first occasion for breaking the now from past and future, and finds a chastened past-ing in detumescence.

Time also plays a decisive role in sexual meeting. This is because sexuality, being an experience of bodyhood, rests on the rhythms of physiological arousal. One's lived movement must be matched with another's. For this reason, the experiences of waiting and hurrying acquire their sexual status as emblems of love. So large are the differences between the usual pace of male and female arousal that in the temporal sphere homosexuality gains an advantage that it has lost to heterosexuality in the spatial doubling of bodyhood.

Waiting on feelings is the lot of both sexuality and love, because feelings are what they are and cannot be pushed by any legislation, however urgent.

Mobilizing sensations can create an embodiment of me or you: I am yours. This leads to many of the phenomena of jealousy: is your body still mine? If it has been another's, are you still mine? Poor humans, caught in sensations that seem for a moment the whole world, have read meaning out of them, and then back in again.

Power and possession, weakness and surrender enter sexual meeting both as imaginative themes for arousal and as actual events that may inhibit arousal. Sexuality thus represents an exquisite balancing act between the demands of imagination and reality. Only the most self-possessed, only those able to be both free and compliant, can afford full conquest or surrender without actual diminution. The danger for the less fortunate is that what can be imaginative play comes to represent actual domination and actual submission.

Similarly, in my seduction of you, I look for signs that you, as much as your body, are aroused. Men and women learn to play on the other's body, hoping that this instrument the body can command the soul. Scruton wrote, "The bodily unity that lies within my grasp is identified in my thinking with another unity, that of the perspective which 'peers' from its face. It is into the well of this perspective that all my desirous gestures are thrown, and I survey its bodily surface for signs of my own significance." Eyes become literally windows of the soul, little able or willing to hide their message of real or incomplete surrender. Thus slave owners searched the faces of their chattels for looks of full obedience.

Here body and soul diverge from one another, so that my capacity to reduce your body to chattel demeans in my eyes your value as a person. Or my capacity to use my body to enslave yours undermines my self-possession through guilt, reducing me. Did the soul emerge as an idea when the body, seemingly conquered through physical power or lust, nevertheless rebelled, perhaps the only remaining signs of life being those soulful, rebellious eyes?

Thus soul appears in sexuality as something to be trampled on or destroyed, as in rape; or cooperatively, in shared moments of delight; or in the experience of melding body and soul, as in romance.

Freud was wise to make sexuality the center of his psychology because of the innumerable ways in which this bodily experience both shapes and is shaped by the psychological. Another example: Wishing can itself become the object of wishing. I may not desire you as much as I wish you to desire me.

Such is the essence of the psychological: the ability to take oneself or others, or any aspect of ourselves and others, as an object. The result is that I hardly see myself or you, only the ideas and images I have formed, my perspective. Magritte put under his picture of a pipe, "This is not a pipe."

But Cézanne did not want to paint pictures. He is rumored to have said he wanted to be like nature and make apples. Why not, since he was part of nature?

Sexuality can be aroused by mere images. Yet it is like nature, able to germinate the real. Is this a trick of nature to propagate the species?

If so, it is a cruel trick. I may propagate the species with someone I hardly know, someone I cannot recognize in the morning.

Or crueler still, parents may be excited by their children, perhaps by images from their own childhood. What sexuality first germinated, sexuality may now use. As a final cruelty this may be the closest both get to a moment of love.

The great engine of life turns on a tiny point that is my point of sight, my perspective. I must train that little light to guide me.

I do not want to be trampled on or destroy;
I want to share myself with you, and nothing
illustrates better the promising, subtle, and
perilous links between body and soul than
the varied history of romance.

What may seem a passionate shared bodyhood in the romantic friendships of youth
proves often the search for a self. Especially
in friendships of the same sex, the worship of
one ideal partner by another reveals the loved
body as chiefly the casing or signature of
what the loving partner would be. The closeness, so seemingly physical, is really an effort
at psychological identification; one party
means to come away transformed by the
other. Then liking is an effort to be like. Insofar as this effort at transformation is successful the person begins to love himself or
herself; the self takes itself as an object of
respect or even adoration rather than hesita-
tion or loathing.

Sexuality serves the same end when one sees oneself mirrored in the aroused astonishment of another. The two processes work best when they work together: then one is loved by someone one wishes to be like. The self wishing to be transformed is seen by the ideal of transformation as already lovable. The danger of becoming like another when one is really not like that other is lessened: individuals can be loved and respect themselves for what they themselves are or can be.

The wonders of idealization and sexuality never cease. The Russians, seeking to shame and blackmail the visiting Indonesian leader Sukharno, gave him Moscow prostitutes and filmed the proceedings. On being shown the films, Sukharno asked for copies so that they could be shown back home. The Indonesian leader knew his power stemmed in part from being a fertility god whose strength sowed the fields.

Men are said to enter relationships most often through sexuality and women through affection. Romance is the opportunity to distribute these interests more equally between the two. It continues even after fusion has passed if both parties find the give-and-take welcome.

Then people learn from one another. It is an exchange of gifts. Couples report that the body can be a loyal friend to such engaged minds. Some women become more sexually adventurous; some men even learn to talk.

But sexuality in long relationships may seem the pursuit of the impossible. A few play out the old ideal of being all-man and all-woman; the ones I know say their minds wander. There is also the exchange of fantasies and images. For some this is a godsend; others find it intrusive on love of one another. I think the luckiest are excited by the body itself: body communes with body while the minds rest.

Or those moving past unfamiliarity, even beyond strangeness and the disfigured, place themselves so firmly, patiently, winningly in the experience of the other that the unfamiliar seems transformed. Do they deceive themselves or was Nietzsche right? He called that emerging beauty of the greatly loved its "thanks for our hospitality."

I know a woman with a withered arm who was so well loved she came to love that once-hated arm; and she herself became more beautiful.

Many more are disillusioned with romance. Then bodyhood, as both desiring and the object of desire, presents a meeting ground that is most simply experienced in masturbation: I give my body pleasure. But this apparently closed circle of bodyhood is still open to self, imagination, and the world. People do not masturbate themselves, in any meaningful sense, any more than they can tickle themselves. The body is the object of desire; yet the necessary intermediary is an imaginative creation or an object endowed with imaginative force, as are fetishistic objects. One does not so much play with oneself as with an image or an object. Perhaps people would be able to make themselves laugh by tickling, as they make themselves climax by masturbation, if an image of someone else tickling them could be sufficiently aroused.

Nevertheless masturbation is a refuge from the world and the vicissitudes of time. Sartre wrote, "An onanist by choice, Genet prefers his own caresses because the enjoyment received coincides with the enjoyment given, the passive moment coincides with the moment of greatest activity: he is at the same time this consciousness which coagulates and this hand which becomes agitated and churns." Those to whom the world and time have given largely pain and humiliation must find this place and moment of satisfaction if they are to survive at all; and the good-hearted may prefer to use themselves rather than to use others. Thus masturbation is a comment on experience at large. The tradition that condemns it is invited to look at the world and times from which it is a refuge. The dignity of masturbation lies in this statement of the dispossessed and all those who know the world.

How long will it take audiences to tire of watching failed romance between people of foolish illusions and impossible personalities? So far is self-possession from being an ideal, even where, as in romance, it is most needed.

Instead there is such an ideal as simultaneous orgasm, humans hoping to master time and physiology in an act of charity or conquest or wonderful fusion. Yet whether as self-possession or the perfect orgasm or enduring romance, this search for ideals remains a central part of the human effort to secure our time and space.

SECURING TIME
AND SPACE

◼

Securing body and self in sexuality is a sensational instance of what life presents as opportunity or disaster in everyday life, for present, future, and past; body, presence, and the world.

◼

In different words, what is it to have a livable human existence? How do I secure what I need, and for those I need?

◼

Enjoying an Italian lunch is to suspend past and future in an extended present. Puritans hurry past it, out of guilt. The greedy cannot secure it either, nervously anticipating its end. And a full present can be emptied by making much of the past: "I remember how these lunches used to be."

The same devices make present horrors bearable. Guilty prisoners get what they feel they deserve. The rest send their minds away, replacing the here and now with pleasant times and places. The pitcher Bill Lee offset the tension of critical moments on the mound by dreaming away. Those who come close to death but survive report leaving their bodies to watch from above. This is security by leaving, as friends accomplish by overlooking an insult.

Sometimes the present is secured by an involuntary minding. Admiral Peary, in search of the South Pole, fell down an ice shaft. He reported looking up to see a narrow slice of blue. At the next moment he experienced the presence of god, which is common for those in extreme danger. God appears, saying, "God is with you," and by an impression radiant and numinous. Peary was not only heartened; he learned how god came by a reputation for omniscience — a voice told Peary that his left boot was unbuckled, which could have cost him his foot. The psychologists say one thing (in extreme danger both our ideals and observing ego scatter, to be experienced outside) and the religious another (god comes when we need him), but the phenomena are unmistakable.

Some are not so lucky: in extremis, evils or devils appear, with demoralization the result.

The present can also be secured by planning or scheming. In war, the time of which is mooded by anticipated danger, the present all but disappears into an intense futuring. Sherman said of Grant that he did not think at all, in the sense of large abstractions or images. When Grant "thought" of Vicksburg and tomorrow, between here and there and now and then a thousand sequential details of supply, movement, minutes, people occurred to him. He lived in these anticipated events, attentions, and orders. He was also said not to "look back." Nor does one simply look forward in such a full futuring: it is more as if one were constantly in the future, though it is only the imagined future. Even such detailed planners as Grant and Napoleon have to wait for the actual future to befall.

Grant shows the human mind as a strong natural event, like a storm or an earthquake. Actually mobilizing the present, it appears to possess the future, carrying others into its purpose on a broad front. This is the nature of willfulness, to make a compact between present and future that at least for a while alters the landscape.

The present can also be secured by slowing it down. Professional basketball players report seeing the plays as if in slow motion. Babe Ruth said he could see the pitched ball approaching him, getting bigger and showing its stitches. There are moments in lovemaking when time stands still.

Some live in a full past. My mother spoke of her father's "anecdotage," a term of endearment and exasperation about his repeated, detailed past-ing. Many feel the way my mother did about the historians of larger landscapes: "Why are they interested in those old times and places?" But a purely antiquarian interest is to be sharply separated from history writing. The latter is as different from anecdotage as Grant's planning is from mania or idle musing. The real historian searches the past with the same intensity Grant brought to the landscape, and for the same reason: there is something vital to be understood. The past is searched like the ground of a future battle because both contain those possibilities of existence that have materialized; in neither case are things known until they are looked for, the real ground separated from what might have been. Historical detail is also "marshaled," with the identical purpose of rescuing the present and preparing for the future.

The historian also finds the past poetic, that is, a stimulus to the imagination, because it contains facts. What really happened collects around itself, in the historian's mind, a world, partly of surmises and reconstructions. Generals and other leaders do the same for the future, to the excitement of their followers. Both these instances denote that the past does not culminate with us here today. Past and future stand as the clearest limits on the terrible egocentricity of the present.

Indeed the evils of the past may little appear in the present but by a sly cunning they decree what we cannot do. So if you chafe before a dull future, look to the past.

We speak of events occurring "in the fullness of time," or bringing forth fruit "in due season," and of aging well, whether wine or people. These all refer to natural processes or cycles that have to be awaited. Even with well-known, repeated cycles, however, there is the experience of waiting in vain; this peach never ripened. After a while, I do not write these paragraphs, they write themselves, the way the Japanese say that you drink the first sake but the first sake drinks the second, and so on. Yet both author and reader wonder if the next paragraph will actually ripen.

In sports, time and space are structured, that is, ruled by agreed-upon meters, minutes, and numbers (here is the court; there are six games to a set). Play occurs within the structures, to indicate what is trespass. We put ourselves inside these conventions, the way we live inside our homes, ceremonies, and careers. All are forms of "making safe" because, for a time and space, the operations of time and space are suspended and replaced.

Trespass in sports takes the form of cheating:
I put aside the rules. As a boy I caddied for
a golfer incapable of hitting the ball out of
a sandtrap; so he threw it. He knew I knew
and I knew he knew I knew. We developed
our own convention within the conventions
of golf. He sought to exchange shame for
pity; I appeared not to notice.

Just as it is possible to live in a full past or
present, so it is possible to make an existence
largely of body, presence, or the world. Loss
of one may be redeemed by extension into
another. Surely Franklin Roosevelt's extraordinary grasp of the world was in part a com-
pensation for his body's crippling and his
loss of love. Or watch timid adolescents filling up their inner worlds.

We seek to secure our existences by medicine, by decoration or concealment, and by ownership, respectively against the vagaries of the body, the dangers of being present in the world, and what the world itself undergoes. Medicine is like a beleaguered garrison, constantly rushing reinforcements to those of its patients endangered afresh by new viruses, environmental insults and accidents, and the changing disharmony of the body. The paradox of medicine is that despite its impressive conquests it does not wither away but quite the contrary grows larger and more ambitious. This is because the enemies of the body are ingenious and ever changing and the means of defense cumbersome and themselves sometimes destructive. As important, medicine becomes institutionalized: it becomes "the body of medicine," which in turn must protect itself, occasionally even at the expense of the body it was begun to protect.

By decoration and concealment I mean the enormous range of clothing, cosmetics, and above all gestures and speech by which we both advance and hide ourselves. These are marks, like tattoos, that express and divert. It is a happy event when the aged dress to express the grandeur of their years and not to pretend youth or hide wrinkles. Yet humans surpass even insects in their gifts for concealment and camouflage. I suspect that such was mind's first duty before the search for warmth, weapons, and transportation. Like the inventions of medicine, however, chameleonship often overcarries, so that while rapid death is the product of openness, a slow death follows giving everything to appearances.

One must dress right among the rich. There are few things they require more.

Contrast presence of mind with presence of body. Just as I need to stand up straight, so I must let my mind be deeply seen only by those who can respect it.

Ownership or possession makes what is perhaps the boldest human claim, to have as one's own. It extends from our thoughts and feelings and acts to that often treasonous site, the body, and beyond, to children, spouses, property, and nations; even the Antarctic and the moon are now claimed, or soon will be. The goals are both enlargement of self and protection from others. The pace varies, from glacial permanence to the transience of titles in athletics, the commodities market, and revolutionary politics. Artists make the supreme claim of ownership, of whole new worlds.

However briefly, suicide may create a future. For a moment the suicidal person imagines the world changed by the act, revenged, redeemed, or escaped from into a fantasy of death.

Mad men and women may also inhabit worlds of their own making, but the joke is, they only pay the rent and the doctor.

The stolen needs to be perceived from the viewpoint of the thieves. Some do not "take" but experience the world as already theirs in movements of wide-ranging spatiality. But much that has been stolen comes to be fully owned when held on to and then brought out in a full, bold presence. In this way, robber barons become the next generation's aristocracy. Such was the experience of the Rockefellers and the Kennedys and is similar to the act of usurpation by which the original artist captures the world's eye, even though that same artist may be first seen as psychotic, and experience life, apart from art, as nowhere and nowhen.

Most, I suspect, would rather own in a tamer way. Perhaps they would prefer to be like happy banks, giving and receiving more, gaining in credit and trust, taking interest.

Reunions are a possibility of human existence that exposes the security or insecurity of one's time and place. One chooses to go back; one enters gradually an old time and place, and without the enhancements of one's presence that familiar, present surroundings may provide. Many would rather wait.

If one was lonely in school, will one be lonely again? Will the other lonely ones return?
Probably not. There is the wish to secure
oneself by possessions, honors, family, titles,
and the chilling awareness of the possibility
of exposure and inferiority. One experiences
the sense of being small again, perhaps
because one is going back to the time and
place of one's smallness: the twin conditions
of the real. What do the arrogant feel? Do
they feel as mean as they can seem?

It is characteristic of the past to hold experience relatively still until it is present-ed.
Thus reunions have the function of "bringing things up to date" or "catching up on
what's happened"; the past is brought back
into the present, shaken, revised. People who
do not go back risk living partly in static,
even dead experience.

The revisited past is found to contain its own future. For example, Brenda was voted most likely to succeed. At the reunion this predicted future confronts the real future: poor Brenda, or happy Brenda, or those happy ones who emerged from the shadows. This going back is also a thrusting forward of a past the future of which is actually here to see.

The revisited past contains, beside its own future, its own past. Only in reuniting may it be possible to ask: "Where were you coming from?" Time has made that clearer and more or less painful. Then each individual coming together is found to have a separate past trailing away on its own, as well as a separate future.

Reunions are spatial as well. We return to a space that is both held in memory and changed. However much or little the buildings and streets have changed, body and presence bear poignant witness to the nature of our biological, human existence. Some classmates are barely recognizable; others step out of the past like talking, moving snapshots. This remembered, beloved person is now a grimacing shell: there seems no one home. That pale memory now presents solidly, with depth and life. Watch on their faces their judgments of you.

MARRIAGE

Marriage is the possibility of human existence in which lived time and space are most extensively shared. Moreover, it declares itself to the world at large and proposes a perhaps indefinite continuance. It is therefore ideally placed to illustrate the extraordinary difficulties in the way of existence, and the various solutions proposed.

In much of the Western world today these difficulties are no longer ones of physical survival and of passing on the germ plasm but instead of psychological survival. In keeping with its psychological task, marriage has become what is called self-conscious: less conventional and more reflective. It is begun later and ended earlier, more thought about and more often dissolved.

Many times marriage starts with a sense of safety and relief. The loneliness of being single, the hazards of seduction or courtship, the narrow social presence of bachelor- or spinsterhood, the question of one's acceptability and lovableness, all these diminish with marriage, even vanish, until the difficulties of being together in more than metered space and time reveal themselves.

These give birth to a sad human cry: "Why must life be so complex?" "Why can't we just exist happily and let each other be?" "Why are even fortunate physical and financial circumstances not enough for life?" Many have blamed neuroticism, others human predation and submission, still others the larger social scene. But it is also possible to point out features of such a widely shared experience that are intrinsically difficult and require ingenuity and persistence for even partial solutions.

The idea of building psychologically is evident in work, art, and science. Marriage is the smallest social unit for building and, like the state, subject to disagreement, rebellion, and civil war. We know that homes can be built together, in both the physical and psychological senses. What does it mean to build a relationship? Or, as is often hoped, "to make a life together"?

Building a relationship or making a life together is to fill shared space and time. This is evident in the accumulated contents of a home, or in the meeting of bodies sexually and in the day-to-day (and in the night-to-night: one wakes in the darkness to find a familiar body there), or in the closeness of related presences: children, relatives, neighbors. These are aspects of spatial building.

One aspect of building a relationship in marriage is the opportunities that shared time and space provide for accumulation. Old couples discover this crowded spatiality when they have to move. It is literally impossible to move. The home has become like the land, geologically impacted, layered, folded. Shafts can be cut, levels exposed; but this much experience does not move.

Another example: People who marry late in life, or remarry, learn that their time and space cannot be simply handed to one another, like a ring. Experience has been built and must be rebuilt. In contrast, it is easier "to start out" together, that is, leave home, begin work, make a dwelling, with all their crises and resolutions.

Building accumulates possessions. It also accumulates talk. Conversation is the verbal form of building together. And, as a rule, people who stop building stop talking.

Building in time is to secure shared memories, a full present, and a future of varied possibilities, but as soon as this is said a problem appears that has defied every philosophical and practical attack. How are we to know the time is shared? One fine morning a spouse awakes to find the other gone: he or she had thought they were together. Such is the very essence of lived time and space: I can be both here (in the sense of clocked and metered time and space) and not here.

Hence nervousness in marriage, and a great deal of destructive fussing. Someone has said that you never know another's marriage, only your own—and only half of that. Paradoxically, this is also the central engine of marital success. Because I can never "know," marriage is inherently unstable and mysterious. And this instability and mystery keeps marriage alive. If I knew that you could never escape me (which sometimes you must do), the possibility of stagnation would loom even larger than it does. The best marriages often seem those in which each party has many times wondered why it should continue one more day. The two minds are free to escape the outermost limits of the relationship and as a result see it, and perhaps decide to make it better. Minds tightly held in loyalty or servitude must lose perspective, strain, and sometimes break.

What is built in time, this relationship that makes part of a life, is precisely the history of experienced crises and resolutions. The sexual act is a bodily metaphor for the experience of possible closeness and climax or distance and disappointment. These are the ways shared time is built: people who share past time recall what they doubted and undertook.

Oddly, failures bring couples closest, because they have signaled what the relationship could bear. And failure, more often than success, deflates vanity, with all its capacity to separate. Failure is also the occasion of humor. Humor, as opposed to wit, indicates the safety one party feels in appearing foolish or awkward in the presence of the other.

Consideration of the personal qualities critical for marriage has entertained authors and readers, playwrights and audiences for centuries. From long before *The Taming of the Shrew*, the vicissitudes of marriage have been explored and imagined into a still-unfolding future that includes *Anna Karenina* and *Arms and the Man*. The record of classical literature supports the record of everyday life: great marriages are no more common than great books or paintings. The rest of us can be forgiven.

The often wild sea-crossing of marriage suggests criteria for crew membership. The fate of those who see marriage as friendship I have sketched already. The fate of those whose expectations are moonlit nights and glamorous seascapes is no different. But even those who love a gale and ascend the mizzenmast in a rolling sea may find themselves tossed overboard. Nor is personal preference or a special itch a more reliable guide; many are recipes for disaster. (My experience is that women are generally better judges than men.) The point is, the qualities necessary in either or both parties are not subject to general laws or prediction. These are what physicists call quantum events, not able to be individually calculated. The most extraordinary disabilities often prove serviceable, and peerless ingenuity, courage, and resilience can become an insufferable bore.

One reason individual traits do not determine success is that, in marriage, perhaps more than in any other relationship, people condition one another. For example, the acquiescent person married to someone aggressive reinforces the aggressiveness. In this way people only a little dominant can gradually become domestic Hitlers.

The ready past-ing of present also transforms spouses. Any present marriage calls
up old family responses; one finds oneself
repeating relationships to parents, siblings,
even to old images of oneself. This transformation of the present gains almost inex-
orable force from the similarity of lived
spaces: my new family is another family, at
least a little like the one I had.

The gay relationships I have known seem no
different. Power or respect, old responses
or new, stagnation or vitality enter with the
same force.

Successful building is therefore an act of will
against the conditionings of past and present.
It means to construct "something of our
own," whether a construction in space, like
a home; or an experience, like an adventure,
that gains its principal reality in time.

In either case, this new act has some of the force of the astonishing, most plainly when a home is built to astound the neighborhood, and more personally when the adventure involves surprise and the spectacular, as is common when people watch sports, read poetry together, go to the theater, or travel.

The search for astonishment dominates human life in innumerable ways. This is evident in the newspapers, entertainment, sports, politics, drama, art, even that most deliberate of activities, science. The hold of magic on the human mind has the same source. Religion and astonishment are deeply intermixed, whether in the personal experience of the numinous or in the gigantic buildings and statues that world religions have scattered everywhere.

The importance of astonishment in ordinary life springs from the need to be moved. One is not to be stagnant, depressed, which is the mood of unchanging time. To this end travel was prescribed for the depressed, or activity of any sort: something is added to experience that leaves us in a different place. Because of the forces of stagnation, the astonishing is needed the way great physical forces are needed in order to move earth and rocks.

One basis for astonishment in marriage is the relationship itself. "Being in love" is its earliest form. Then the most commonplace features and events astonish. The grossest overestimation of the other, toward which the term *idealization* reaches, transforms the presence and body of the beloved, including whatever objects in space are close by. This overestimation is accompanied by a depletion or humbling of the loving one, like a courtier before a king. The term *moving* does not do justice to the profound transformation of energies and values involved.

Time is transformed as much. Anticipation of the beloved becomes an exquisite amalgam of agony and joy. The mood of meeting remains a predictable altar for the poetic imaginations of every age. And the past remembering of an old love is a torch-point to which the most depleted spirits return with a kind of luminescence.

Wise people exploit the power of movement of being in love to take them to a new place, as in marriage, to new dwellings and relationships. There are not many such forces.

Being in love passes, as a rule, in weeks or months. Then the couple either stagnates or seeks one of the forms of relationship that secure astonishment over longer periods. I believe the commonest of these has been adoration: One of the two parties is elevated to a godlike status, for example the man as monarch, the woman flatterer, court, and servant. (This gains force from the prevailing sexual inequality in our culture.) Or the man is all-man and the woman is all-woman, in a rite of sexual worship. Such an elevation is really an institutionalization, like monarchy or marriage itself, of sentiments that may have occurred before.

Yet genuine adoration can seldom survive familiarity, at least when the adorer is valued chiefly for adoring. Institutionalized adoration is therefore self-defeating unless the two parties are willing to undertake lifelong acting assignments out of tradition or calculation.

Another solution partakes of being in love, institutionalized adoration, and respect. This is the idea of putting each other first. Putting the other first is a durable remainder of the once-intoxicating love; and it substitutes for mutual adoration the livable ideal of mutual priority. It also draws an element of astonishment from the implied combination of idealization and respect. The capacity for idealization that every hopeful person carries can be transmitted to the other and by the mutuality of that effort made available to the relationship at large. Respect tempers both the distortion and control that idealization can produce by asserting: I also take you as you are. This joint conveyance of idealization and respect, of devotion to the other's future as well as present, is an astonishing experience.

Hegel wrote that no man is a hero to his valet because the valet is a valet. The capacity to idealize is what elevates people above valets.

The result is, one gives to another, and when mutually administered, receives back, possibilities for the future that by dint of belief and striving can have surprising results. And when these results are not immediately obvious, in fact to other eyes improbable, they are performative simply by being hoped for. Marriage begins with a performative, "I pronounce you man and wife," which creates a fact by being spoken, like the umpire's "in" or "out", or the name I was given that tells me who I am. Marriage can continue with another performative: "I believe in you." It is as if the parties are renamed in the light of each other's convictions, however long that takes to complete itself and however incompletely the result is effected.

Being in love mobilizes and focuses attention. Time, and often marriage, dissipate it. Even deep, vital people can become serviceable sticks of furniture. As a result, the first mission of a mutual priority is the ordering of attention: in our space I give you my time. And unlike the student or the reader, the committed mind wanders at its peril; it had better return something to the relationship. That something may only be the fact of attention itself, which under many circumstances is astonishing.

Attention is the first step toward what Conrad called "the intimate felicities of daily affection," which is as vital to psychological being as oxygen is to the body. It may also be as invisible as oxygen to any but the most careful observers, only making itself known in its absence.

Yet after all this talk of attention and astonishment the most important test of marriage may be this: How many times did each party go to sleep without saying that awful thing each wanted to say?

Because marriage is a state without a constitution, even the most determined attention or wisest counsel cannot be effective if the power held in marriage is not checked by something like a constitutional rule. Marriage, as much as the successful nation, needs a means of balancing power, if the extraordinary demands on a continuing relationship are not to end in tyranny and enslavement.

A mutual priority balances power, with the result that each must manage both himself or herself and the other. Congress and the presidency are stalemated; the only recourse is negotiation and eventually compromise. It is the very finality of both authorities that gives good sense a chance to prevail.

Once wives were often managed but not respected and husbands respected but not managed. Today the economic power of men tends to be pitted against the emotional power of women. Nevertheless, management enters marriage as a frequently alien ideal because good spirits hope to prevail by goodness and authoritarian spirits hope to prevail by their power. And there are many who believe that love conquers all. May some good lord protect each one.

Negotiation and management are natural responses to stalemate, but not the only ones. However superior stalemate is to checkmate, it suggests stale mates, a radical loss of movement. Happily, people who share each other's space and time cannot remain still long. Explosions are the natural result of being stuck so close while neither surrendered nor moved. The vehicle of deliverance is free speech, the constitutional prerogative of mutual authority. Speech is even freer in marriage than it is in the state. For example, permission is granted to shout "Fire!" in a burning home.

One theme of marital quarrels is often misunderstood. Desperate spouses fall back on an old source of power: The invocation of a third party, an old lover or a parent, as agent of jealousy or support (this pattern was learned in dealing with mother and father). It is not pathological when really needed. The issue frequently is: Do you care enough to fight?

Quarrels between equal parties end either in departure or what is called reflection. In view of the other's authority one must leave or "double back on oneself," that is, take in some hitherto unacknowledged aspect of the other's time and space as it has experienced yours. Typically this results in "feeling bad" as the painful aspect of the other's experience is shared. Apology can result, but more important the enlargement of shared experience, which is called understanding. Then the other has the chance to "accept" the apology, perhaps perfunctorily but ideally with an enlargement of that person's understanding, too. Mistakes are to be seen as natural. One seldom learns without making them.

A deeper principle of family life may, however, be the principle Aristotle put at the heart of the state. Logic and reason, he suggested, are powerless when quarrels reach the highest levels of politics. The only recourse is confusion, with its opportunities for time and chance to intervene. In the absence of such saving confusion, the family may have to go to bed.

Marriage has been called a great cage with everyone on the outside trying to get in and everyone on the inside trying to get out. This is not the whole story. But it is true enough to pay off the psychotherapist's mortgage.

DIVORCE

Just as many get in, many get out. Then the metaphor of the cage referred to in the last chapter collapses, because divorce means the rending of the largest space and time humans share. As a result there are few easy divorces; there is only the possibility of learning and renewal.

Not many can be so buoyant as Margaret Mead, who announced that she had had three happy marriages. Anthropologists of Margaret Mead would like to hear from the husbands.

Space says it first, in an emptied house. What had been occupied however unhappily, is now still. Then humans discover they can be as much alive to one another in footsteps and rustlings, the closing of a cabinet door, as in many of the passionate happenings of life. And the home may be emptied in another way: the one left may send his or her imagination where the other has gone, so there is really no one home. "One less egg to boil, one less plate to clean," the saying goes, but on a dying note.

The one leaving steps into a world both alive with possibility and curiously forlorn. This is because the leave-taking is for a long time only a movement in metered and dated space and time. The boldest and least regretful imaginations still turn back, not only or chiefly in guilt, but because the past grips. Changed circumstances are reminders by their very differences, even very happy differences.

Time reveals a feature of experience perhaps encountered on no other occasion. For the one who goes, time is accelerated; for the one who stays, it is slowed or stopped. The act of separation has pushed one into the future and the other into the past. The rending of shared time and space has separated their lived times as much as their spaces.

Many also discover that what they wanted least is what they need most. This may be hard to admit, especially if vindictiveness prevails. Women are said to do better alone than men, perhaps because they are less really alone in our competitive culture, and they are the ones most often left. But divorced women have thrust upon them what this culture neglects for women: the need for independence and authority.

Divorce is difficult in the same way marriage is difficult: it opens out onto fresh ground. As long as divorce is trivialized in the same way marriage is trivialized—by seeing it as two people joining or parting—it must be not only difficult but impossible. As marriage means building a new time and space, so does divorce, if it is not to mean regret and death.

Again like marriage, divorce secures its covenants from the limits it puts on the future. At present these concern chiefly income, property, and custody—as usual, what can be counted, like money and days. These possessions, and division of possessions in quantifiable space and time, repeat the first steps of marriage in which people share property and paychecks. The transformation of lived space and time may or may not follow, or precede. My mother remained married to my father for long after they were divorced. Indeed it was easier to be married to him when he wasn't around. She went right on building the home they started together as if he were gone for a weekend.

This is to say that divorce may be the continuance of marriage under changed conditions, sometimes but not always the reverse of the way war is the continuance of politics. I believe it is important to acknowledge this possibility, lest people expect too much new of divorce as they may have expected too much new of marriage. Humans are capable of continuing what they were doing under the most extraordinarily different circumstances, in apparent obliviousness of night or arctic air.

Divorce is susceptible to these silent continuances because it is so little presided over by ceremony and celebration. The realization of marriage begins for many only at the altar, and that fails to penetrate the lived experience of not a few. The present begun in marriage can continue indefinitely despite divorce until some milestone pasts the futureless, perhaps the death of the departed spouse. The tragedy of divorce is not so much the end of marriage — which may never have begun — but this ease of endlessness.

When divorce was shameful and unmentionable, the ease was greatest. Nowadays psychotherapists, group meetings, every magazine and newspaper cry up divorce, so there is less chance of it slipping by unnoticed. Soon we will institutionalize divorce. The churches and city halls of the future will discover solemn rites, separating past and future, protecting children, commemorating ends as well as beginnings, above all sanctifying what is serious. A human society cannot afford to live in public shame.

I doubt this will undermine marriage where it is not undermined already. Nietzsche wrote, "It was only by the thought of suicide that I got through many a dark night." The thought of divorce, like the thought of suicide, can lighten the present, lend independence to the spirit, and thrusting aside imprisonment, freshen the urge to try again.

The rites of marriage do not make marriage easier, but more formidable. They make it harder to "slip into" marriage. The same could be true of divorce.

Here is a possible ceremony of divorce: "Do you take this spouse as your former spouse, for better or for worse: to be met at every graduation, marriage, and funeral; to be, like you, capable of error and deceit, deeper understanding than you recognize, wiser judgment than present opinions would allow; to honor what is honorable, remember what was good, forgive what was not, and support one another whenever possible in the remaining races to be run?"

Such will seem as far-fetched to many present couples as their wedding vows would have seemed to the caveman dragging off his mate.

CHILDREN

Just as the national state must move from being a device for the conquest and possession of physical space and its assurance over time, the family has to find its means of psychological development and propagation, married or divorced. With it come the divergent possibilities of psychological possession and liberation.

These possibilities are plainest in the rearing of children. Every family decides whether children are to be like conquered possessions, colonized by imported regulations and ideals, or independent, human centers of time and space allowed a respectful development of their own. The latter is not a recipe for anarchy because the new citizens must also learn to respect the old ones.

In fact, the free, rich rearing of children must be a dance of alternating restriction and encouragement. Much as we love them, they have to get on with us. Let them be confused. We are too, we adults who have to find our way between freedom and compliance.

The most powerful modern devices for the colonization of children are theories of development. When so-called developmental stages are seen as like the physical growth of the embryo—in Erikson's words, "In the sequence of significant experiences, the healthy child, if properly guided, can be trusted to conform to the epigenetic laws of development"—then a mighty tool of control and distortion is at hand. This is not to deny that human growth may occur stepwise, or that there is much to be usefully learned by studying children in the course of their growth. What we cannot say is whether that stepwise growth is inherent in the body or, in contrast, is at least partly an imposition of the cultural world around. The point is, any theory of development presented as law operates like the legal system, as an instrument of social expectation and control.

Yet no matter how many instances of police brutality are reported, almost no one wants to be without the policeman. And no one who has reared children has avoided being the policeman. Further, the need for the enforcement of rules of respectful conduct extends beyond keeping the peace. Children do not always know what to eat or how to learn. Only a foolish parent would throw away the accumulated knowledge of those subjects to "let the child learn on his or her own." The free society, what we can call the society as conversation, has precisely as its central topic of conversation this issue: When does my influence on you, however well intended, go over into distortion and diminution?

Society cannot hold such a conversation without free speech, which is the social form of free imagination. But just as the rights of children are poorly defined and defended in the law, so no constitutional rule protects free speech in the family. In fact a kind of sovereignty prevails there, by which parents know best.

"Don't complain," "don't worry," the parents say, looking plaintive and worried.

Yet it is often true that the children are worried about the parents! And not just because they are dependent on them.

Free speech occurs in most families the way it occurs in countries where democracy is an opportunity for disorder. Consider breakfast or dinner in even happy homes. Then free speech invites a military takeover. The constitutional goal of free speech is different: not only are individual points of view protected, an opportunity is provided for discourse, out of which apparently intractable and divisive issues can be resolved.

Free speech in a happy family is like a stew bubbling in a cauldron. Everything gets thrown in and the result is delicious. Nowhere are the social possibilities of existence better realized. The closeness of feeling and the freedom of expression produce what is usually possible nowhere but in the individual creative mind: that flow of time and space which is delightful and altogether unpredictable. And the degree of family delight is matched only by the extent to which it is ephemeral and unrecorded—a result at once unforgettable and gone forever.

This is the experience of children in the luck-iest families. It does not extend into adult-hood. Then returning children learn the three-day rule: Happiness at being back lasts about that long. At that point, parents resent boarding and feeding grown relatives and the children resent the obligations incurred.

The right to speak is the first order of per-sonal emancipation. On this point the state and family converge. But in the family free speech requires a turning-upside-down of the usual systems of developmental evaluation. Specifically it means that children may be right, not just right in their imaginative play but in what they see and want. The cate-gories *childish* and *immature* denote not only dependency but unreliability. As long as they dominate the judgments adults make of chil-dren, the possibility of free speech must be remote.

In different words, the other side of free speech is respectful listening, which is far more important in the family than it is in the state. The reason for this is central. We do not put people in jail for failing to listen because the state declares that it is just as important to be able to close your ears as to be able to open your mouth. The free state is a large conversation and no one can be expected to hear everything. On the other hand, the family is small conversations: not listening is rudeness, disrespect.

I believe that free speech has been only slowly extended to the family for a reason that exists apart from the usual talk of immaturity and guided development. Marriage in the presence of children means sharing space and time with a stranger, albeit someone who, like the future, is an intimate stranger. The dice game of genetic mixing (which so often makes a child closer to one parent than another and divides families) means that each child is actually neither one parent nor the other and, more than that, is a child, that strange, small, growing thing, wonderful but with demonstrated gifts for monstrosity. In addition, children think of themselves as grown-up, often more grown-up than their elders and usually more so than their youngers, just as adults do. Hence the naturalization papers are slow to come.

Adoption and blended families are still more random experiments of genetic and family mixing. Then the institution's capacity for self-discovery and freedom is even more sorely tried. Yet the wisest parents know more parents are needed than most children can find at home. We all need to pick up bits and pieces from each other, often large pieces, for the rest of our lives.

Many children grow up among adults no better than uncaged beasts. Adulthood confers powers and rights met nowhere but in war. These children learn the wary behavior of people in such dangerous and unpredictable environments: it is not safe to notice or not to notice.

Naturalization and freedom stand at one end, possession and tyranny at the other. The latter remains the rule because childhood still has the status of slavery: Everyone speaks of "their" children the way they speak of "their" cars. We grow up possessed, and then wake to wonder whose those strange inner voices are.

THE SEARCH
FOR THE REAL

When you trespass, what do I lose? What is
a human or psychological loss? Minimally
my space and time, more deeply my hope or
love or even myself.

Then something about me, perhaps psyche
or soul or my humanity, appears diminished
or even squeezed out. What is this fragile
psyche that otherwise takes its place at the
very head of the class, as in *psychological* or *psychiatric*?

I would like to "be somebody." But will that
somebody be me? How can I tell? The
Buddhists teach the self is both here and
not here. Look for it in the stream of con-

sciousness and it is hard to find. On the other hand, my names, roles, relationships define me; I even take on an "identity." Look me up in the phone book—you will find me there. Yet is that "really me"?

※

As I can seem real, so I can seem unreal. This extends beyond feelings of unreality or dreaminess into everyday experiences of asking, "Did I do that?" "Was that me?" Here we enter the territories of possession and self-possession, of owning or not owning one's "own" emotions and ideals.

※

I also want to acknowledge you. How do I know if you are here? Pooh asked if Piglet was home. Piglet answered no. That puzzled the slow Pooh, but it is an everyday puzzle to the rest of us, because you too can be real or unreal. If I am going to marry you or lend you money, I need to know.

NAMING

Am I Leston Havens? Am I my own name, with its particular experiences and family connections? My mother wanted to call me Tristram, after her dead brother who in turn had been named after my grandfather's favorite book, *Tristram Shandy*. Leston seemed to me a small improvement. I was Lester Depester in elementary school, and after that Lester, Liston—nobody could get it right. Is that who I am? The father of a friend always called me Mike, hoping, I suppose, to reduce my fanciness. I have never met anyone else called Leston. On my own (as is said), I tacked on *Doctor*, which they let us wear on most occasions. That felt better. Many people have changed their whole names, to bring them into closer connection with what they feel about themselves or want to be. Marriage means a change of name to many more—she becomes him—as if wives were only first names, Kit or Muffy, like slaves in plantation households. I once worked for a splendid man—the only child of a proud, colorful father—who was named Harry Caesar Solomon, three kings indeed! I do not know what he felt about his name, but he could have worn it like a flag.

Naming is the first moment of social invasion, into that still-unformed experience of oneself, that first delicate time and space of our own. We are now officially theirs, with only a starting little moniker of our own, often less distinctive than a stone. Joe they could have called me, or Bill—names everywhere. Either would have safely hid me, perhaps for a lifetime.

Rarely today, you meet someone who started out unnamed—orphaned, most likely, and unwanted. One man I knew felt that particular indefiniteness all his life. Eventually he was named, by a foster family, and that name stuck. But he never felt he knew who he was; there was always a moment when he heard his name called in which he had to remember, "That is me."

More often you meet people who were given one set of names at birth and then another when adopted. It is a curious experience to learn, usually much later, that you are "really" someone else. Life takes on a split focus.

We are given many other names as we grow older, most decisively by peers when we learn we are big or small, smart or dumb, or worst of all, weird or crazy. These are the performatives of fate, sometimes with us forever.

Freud said anatomy was destiny, Sullivan said society was destiny, Binswanger said purpose was destiny, but often these names are destiny, however much they may be shaped by anatomy, society, and purpose. And it never stops, until we become like English princes, one long string of names.

Some are overwhelmed early. I know a man who is the son of a famous murderer, or so the courts decided. The son has the same names as his father. No one meets the son as he is: everyone's mind is filled with memories of the father so often in newspapers and magazines. There is a great past-ing and mistaking. This is the common experience of famous people's children. No wonder many are driven to outrageous acts of individuation, if not to total oblivion.

The convicted man's son made the best of it, spending his life in defense of the father. Strange things happened. Another famous murder occurred in which one of his names figured. And a writer, perhaps seeking to make himself known, took the father's name. Here was a fresh invasion. Let the writer have it, one might say. But there was almost nothing else the son had left.

Psychiatry is a great namer. Patients are psychotic, neurotic, schizophrenic, paranoid, obsessive, psychopathic. This is not the standard medical practice, in which one has cancer of the liver or an infection of the brain. Psychiatric names attach to the whole person, as is true of the names people call each other when they're angry. I ask, is the patient all schizophrenic or all neurotic; is it like pregnancy? Once medicine did the same thing: you were febrile or chlorotic.

People care very much who they are. Even people who say they're nobodies give it a ring of distinction. And people who really appear to be nowhere and nowhen avoid describing themselves at all. We speak of "lost souls."

Others go about collecting names the way some collect china or paintings. I know a man who founds societies and then is president and honorary president and president emeritus, the way kings used to do. The danger here is the danger of success everywhere: the man I know became so full of himself he is insufferable. Here self-possession is blown up into the caricature of a person. One result is that he possesses more the titles than himself.

Many famous people gain psychological weight. Not only do they seem weighty to others, but famous people often live in a self-contemplation of titles and prizes that displace the lightness of being. There are also those who "drop" names, gaining weight by taking bits of fame onto themselves. In either case, it is a sad property of being to be easily displaced: a title offers a handier, more secure point of existence that thrusts aside the person. Titles fill up a person the way tree stumps clog a stream.

Watch on a hospital ward the staff's treatment of the famous. It is all "sicklied over" with deference or defiance. The name drives out others' souls, too, this one hopeful, that one withdrawn.

Often failure is a surer road to self-possession than is success. Failure strips a person of
names, and the individual left may be oneself.
Nothing so announces the presence of a person as those saddest credentials, suffering
and pain. Yet many would like an easier road
to self-possession, one not paved with misery
and defeat.

Obstructions that road will surely have and
at least the appearance of defeats, because
humans can always see obstructions as defeats, even when a clear path lies beyond
them. That is both the good news and the
bad, our nature being as remarkably able to
turn forebodings into triumphs as into dis-
asters. And it is one of the paradoxes of the
human that often we do not arrange the tri-
umph until we have imagined the disaster.

THE REAL

The sincerity of a Cézanne painting springs from its creation of real space and time. The paintings are given weight, gravity, as well as life and charm, and duration of mind which is manifest by a certain mood. These are qualities we wish as much from people. We speak of bringing out from nature or others what is experienced as real.

The best human encounters can be like such painting, aimed at revelation of the individual motif. We are not drawing a picture of someone, but allowing the emergence, necessarily incomplete and changing, of something real or authentic. I have said Cézanne wanted to be nature, not to paint it, to be able to produce beauty, weight, reality, as nature does.

These paintings and people are of greater interest to us than many natural events because they are produced by minds and times like our own. They are creative acts, by which is meant bringing out, making real, creating something new as a result of meeting. What does one bring out? Color, solidity, internal harmony amid conflict, a dynamic relationship with the world. In the same way the healthy body is set forth in medicine as something the whole enterprise of treatment looks for and celebrates.

Hear what musicians and other composers said of Mozart's music. Frederica von Stade spoke of its "emotional truthfulness" filling every page. Richard Westenburg wrote, "Every happy musical idea of Mozart contains some thread of sadness; and every 'sad' idea bears some measure of hope. This could be a partial clue, at least, to the humanity we sense in him." Recall Joyce's "laughtears." A harmony of conflict we can say: nothing human is alien.

Then Artur Schnabel's sentences: "The so-
natas of Mozart are unique; they are too easy
for children and too difficult for artists." The
human is easy for children, perhaps because
still unconflicted. But later, for any of us to
include it all—that may seem impossible!

Is this what we sense in the real: both the
directness of nature and its many-sidedness,
inexhaustibility?

Robert Schumann remarked that Mozart's
music became fresher and fresher the more
he heard it. What is this, so different from
our experience of the familiar, mother of
contempt? Could it be the real is defined just
so: able to push aside the clichés that have
supplanted us, to be experienced more and
more as we encounter it?

But the real can emerge from the artificial too. Yourcenar has her dying prostitute put on a fake smile and then, seeing herself in a mirror, smile at the successful fiction.

It is said Cézanne held the motif (from nature) in his mind until it worked on his emotional apprehension of the scene, which in turn generated movement of paint onto canvas, resulting in the apples. The apprehension and movement had to get past his artistic conscience, which decided whether apprehension and movement were faithful to the motif or the result of preconceptions and clichés. We can imagine a neurophysiology of this effort in which preconceptions are warded off as the new material makes its way through the brain.

Perhaps it is important that both Mozart and Cézanne claimed to have an apprehension of the whole piece of music or painting, so that the final effector stage of movement, of notes or paint onto paper or canvas, was done from a completed apprehension.

I predict the time is not far off when the real will appear on another kind of screen. The brain coming together in a complex harmony must reveal itself to the subtle measures of our expanding chemistry and physics. It will be a great blessing for children. Let the impossible parent appear; watch the child's harmony disperse. Once medicine could not believe that parents broke their children's bones either, until Kempe's X-rays proved it.

But now the self-possessed do not possess anything they can measure or time. They do wonder how long they can go without losing their mind or at least their temper. Having been around themselves many years they are not surprised.

They know that everyone has much to forgive himself or herself for. But not to forget: It is only by a keen awareness of our worst proclivities that we are kept from repeating them.

The prevailing irony of psychological life is this secrecy of the obvious. We are citizens of a vast republic in which each man and woman breathes secretly and ashamed the same forbidden air. Even the dreadful trauma and varieties of human lots that move experience beyond the wildest reaches of the novelist's imagination still ground themselves in a common soil.

This is what gives good people their similarity: They have come to be at peace with their human nature; they have come into possession of themselves. The finest often seem ordinary or simple because they are simply human. Such is the paradox of individuation: the time arrives when we individuate into one another.

My soul is at bottom like my body. Most of it is already in the textbooks. When the surgeon or the therapist opens me up, what each sees is pretty much what everyone has. So much for the mysterious and unique human spirit. As for professionals, what I care about is how they open me up and what they do when they're inside.

Can they keep me alive? Can they bring me to life? For a while.

DEATH AND DYING

Plato recommended that we practice dying. He must have had a protected life. Many of us began practicing early when people we needed left or died and our world collapsed. I cannot imagine my own death will seem very important to me now.

It is true I have been lucky, with a remarkable family and friends, the most interesting work in the world, and a body that held up for many decades. I have lived much more than I expected, which, I believe, is what makes death bearable. But I do not mean I take myself as lightly as I would like.

Hearing Desmond Tutu speak, I realized the truth of a friend's quotation: Angels can fly because they take themselves lightly. Tutu said, with Secret Service people standing by, that he must go back to South Africa immediately. His wife had said so. Since coming to America, she told him, he had been made a bishop and won the "Nobel thing"; when she woke in the morning, she felt like she had been sleeping with the Pope. He seemed to me truly light as he told this serious joke upon himself, in the shadows of the watchful men assigned to protect him from assassination.

I would like to be like that, close to the facts, not weighed down with self-importance. I can read a paragraph of Conrad and see how close to human truth some stay. I wish I could carry my ideal simply as an ideal, like Tutu, and let my striving be just that, a striving.

Now poor Tutu may have to reach a still-more-perilous striving—to place himself between the blacks and whites, the first understandably enraged and the second so guilty, in order to show that respect must go everywhere.

Nietzsche had the extraordinary notion that we should ask of our lives if we would live them over and over again, with nothing changed. He, like most of us I expect, was repulsed by the idea, but the question became a test. If we have used our experience to fashion a viable existence we owe that result in part to the experience and should be grateful not only for the viable existence but also for the past, however painful, from which it came. Many would exclaim, there must be an easier way! But there may not be.

I wonder if this is the reason the greatest stories are told and read over and over again, because the result justifies the pain. And why these same stories must be rewritten for every age so we can see that they may be our stories too.

A man appeared to have died during a difficult journey far from home. He was half-buried by the roadside, but in fact had not died, recovered and very slowly made his way back. He was not well received. They had mourned him as dead; now he had returned, and they had already divided his possessions.

To the old I say, in order to preserve a viable existence, keep your wills a little secret. As what attractiveness your character had lessens and you become more and more a burden, keep the power you have, right to the end, so they will protect you in the belly of the whale.

If anyone asks whether god exists, perhaps you should answer as Gandhi did when he was asked what he thought of western civilization: "That would be a good idea." Humans are a colossal discordant family much in need of a good mother and father; meanwhile, we may not be wise to assume that there is someone beside ourselves who will save us. For many of those I have admired most, religion is the history of human wisdom and folly to be rethought by every age and people so they can take possession of themselves, free and compliant. Can we, as well, travel that human ground in such a way we open ourselves to what it teaches and use its collisions not as a spur to revenge but to fashion a life that can be lived? And a death that can be died with only those regrets that signal hopes we need never have had?

We will have caught a glimpse of each other and ourselves, a sigh, a smile that link us all together on the human ground, the dead to the living and the living to the unborn.